MW01097062

Hand Lettering God's Word

JENNY HIGHSMITH

HARVEST HOUSE PUBLISHERS
EUGENE, OREGON

Unless otherwise indicated, all Scripture quotations are taken from the Holy Bible, New International Version®, NIV®. Copyright © 1973, 1978, 1984, 2011 by Biblica, Inc.® Used by permission. All rights reserved worldwide.

Verses marked ESV are from The ESV® Bible (The Holy Bible, English Standard Version®), copyright © 2001 by Crossway, a publishing ministry of Good News Publishers. Used by permission. All rights reserved.

Verses marked NLT are taken from the Holy Bible, New Living Translation, copyright © 1996, 2004, 2015 by Tyndale House Foundation. Used by permission of Tyndale House Publishers, Inc., Carol Stream, Illinois 60188. All rights reserved.

Verses marked BSB are taken from The Holy Bible, Berean Study Bible, copyright © 2016, 2018 by Bible Hub. Used by Permission. All Rights Reserved Worldwide.

Verses marked NRSV are taken from the New Revised Standard Version of the Bible, copyright © 1989 by the Division of Christian Education of the National Council of the Churches of Christ in the USA. Used by permission. All rights reserved.

Verses marked CEV are taken from the Contemporary English Version, copyright © 1991, 1992, 1995 by American Bible Society. Used by permission.

Cover design by Nicole Dougherty
Interior design by Faceout Studio, Lindy Martin
Front cover photo, watercolor, and hand lettering by Jenny Highsmith

Hand Lettering God's Word
Copyright © 2020 by Jenny Highsmith
Published by Harvest House Publishers
Eugene, Oregon 97408
www.harvesthousepublishers.com

ISBN 978-0-7369-7817-0 (pbk.)

All rights reserved. No part of this publication may be reproduced, stored in a retrieval system, or transmitted in any form or by any means—electronic, mechanical, digital, photocopy, recording, or any other—except for brief quotations in printed reviews, without the prior permission of the publisher.

Printed in South Korea

21 22 23 24 25 26 27 28 / FCSK - FO / 10 9 8 7 6 5 4 3 2

Soli Deo Gloria!

TO GOD BE THE GLORY

To Drew, thank you for encouraging me in my passions and loving me through my struggles. You've always fought for me—believing in me and my abilities and spurring me on toward the person God created me to become. I love you.

To my parents, thank you for your words of wisdom and for watching the kids so that I could write. Mom, thank you for inspiring my crafty, creative side with all the fun projects we've completed together. Daddy, thank you for your many talks on spiritual and personal growth that have inspired me toward a deeper relationship with Christ.

To my art teachers, Mrs. Moran and Mrs. Johnson, thank you for being my first sources of artistic inspiration. Thank you for encouraging me to pursue art and showing me how much joy can be found in creating.

To Heather, thank you for thinking of me and giving me the opportunity to write this book. It is a lifelong dream come true.

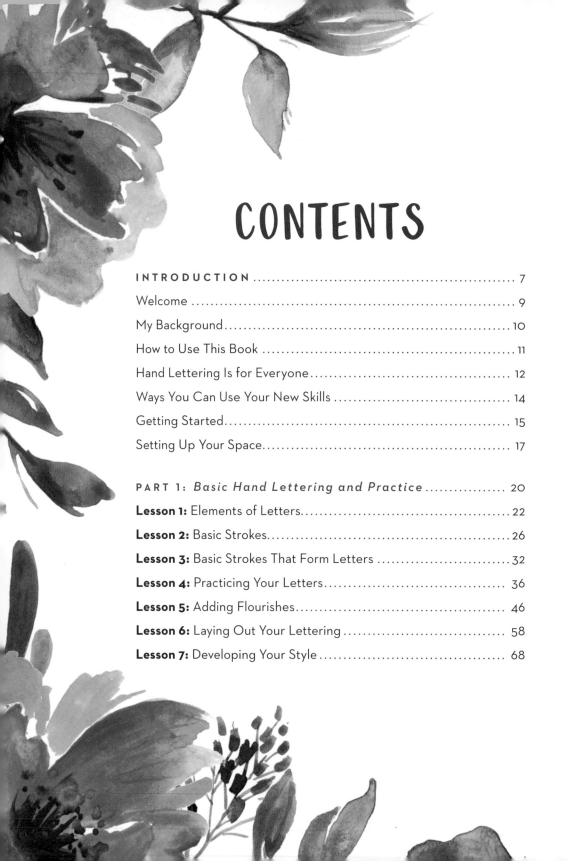

CONTENTS

Introduction

WELCOME

It all began with a desire to remind myself of God's truth. When I started my hand lettering journey six years ago, I was looking for a way to write truth beautifully and be reminded of it every day. I wanted to read truth when I looked in the mirror, when I was making dinner, and whenever I was distracted around my house. My mind tends to be at war with itself—convincing me that I am less than what God has created me to be. That my worth is defined by my striving and what I've achieved. That it is impossible for God to love me because I'm lacking. So I set out on a mission to surround myself with truth and make the process an outlet and the result beautiful. Because that's exactly what truth is: beautiful.

As my purpose became clear, I discovered a love for lettering that quickly turned into a passion and, eventually, due to high demand, a business. I opened an online shop, began teaching workshops, and designed an online class so anyone could learn to letter. The process of creating something beautiful by hand takes time and dedication. And, for me, it has always been something I have used to worship God and experience His presence. I hope that as you learn the art of lettering, you are able to quiet your mind and focus on the One your soul longs for—the One who gives you life and completes you.

As you go through each chapter, I encourage you to slow down, remove distractions, and meditate on the beauty of God's presence and the truth of His Word. I pray that by the end of this book, not only will you have learned a skill that will bring you joy, but you will also know how deep His love is for you and will have experienced peace in His presence and redemption in His truths over your life.

Blessings,

MY BACKGROUND

I have been in art classes since I was eight years old. As a child, I went to art camps and took every opportunity I had to practice my skills. In high school, I took advanced art classes and started selling portraits my junior year. I sold more than a dozen portraits before graduating. In college, I continued to paint and draw—more for my own pleasure—and decided that pursuing a degree in visual communications was the way I wanted to go. I enjoyed working on the school yearbook, learning how to lay out magazines, and discovering how to turn my artwork into digital media through Photoshop, Illustrator, InDesign, and Dreamweaver.

This was helpful to me when my best friend and I started our own graphic design business. During that time, I also began hand lettering—creating art prints for friends and family—and experimenting with canvas, markers, and watercolors. I never considered myself a calligrapher. I didn't buy the fancy feathers or messy inkwells, and I didn't take any classes. I just began developing my own style, and people started asking me if they could buy what I created.

Then I was asked to become a wholesale artist for a storefront. It was at this point that I realized I had found something I loved doing and people wanted, so I worked hard to perfect my skills and acquire the best materials. My canvases were expensive for me to create and for others to purchase, so I looked for a less expensive option so that everyone could have my artwork. Eventually I began digitizing my artwork and creating the eight-by-ten-inch art prints you see in my shop now.

HOW TO USE THIS BOOK

This book is divided into two parts. The first part provides instructions on the fundamentals of hand lettering and practical tips for creating a beautiful style. The second part goes more in depth on hand lettering each individual letter of the alphabet and includes a Scripture reference that starts with that letter, as well as a short devotion. My heart for this book is that you would use the first part to get the basics of hand lettering down so that in the second part you can use your new skills to help you memorize and meditate on God's Word.

I would encourage you to take each chapter slowly, maybe a day or even a week at a time. It might be tempting to rush through the book. Don't rush! Slow down and really enjoy the process.

The spaces in this book are meant for you to write in and practice your skills. If for any reason you are hesitant or feel you need extra room, you can always download copies of the practice sheets here: **www.jennyhighsmith.com/practice-sheets.** Or you could use tracing paper over the practice pages in this book. This might help you not be as worried about hand lettering perfectly.

HAND LETTERING IS FOR EVERYONE

Whether you're an experienced artist or someone who just likes to doodle, hand lettering is all about your specific style. When I first started lettering, my style was completely different than it is now. It took time to develop and evolve my style, so don't be intimidated. You can do this! I am going to make sure you are comfortable and you walk away feeling confident in your own unique lettering style and prepared with all the tools and resources you need to continue practicing.

To give you an example of how someone's personal style changes and improves over time, I've included three photos showing you how my hand lettering started off, how it looked about a year into my lettering journey, and how my current style looks today.

MY FIRST PRINTS   **ONE YEAR IN**

be an
encourager
the world
has enough
critics

WAYS YOU CAN USE YOUR NEW SKILLS

No matter what you decide to do with your hand-lettering skills, there are a lot of fun, unique options out there. Check out some of my favorite ideas and DIYs:

• Make personalized gifts for friends and family during the holidays.

• Decorate your home with favorite quotes and lyrics by creating your own artwork.

• Create beautiful signage for baby showers, wedding showers, birthdays, and special events.

• Design your own wedding invitations and signs.

• Apply your lettering to your graphic design portfolio.

• Learn how to create your own script fonts.

• Letter on various materials and objects like canvas, fabric, chalkboards, globes, lamps, storage boxes...anything!

• Take your Instagram profile to the next level by creating beautiful overlays for your photos.

• Apply what you learn to your scrapbooking to add a personal and unique touch. The possibilities are endless.

GETTING STARTED

MY GOAL

My goal is to teach you all the skills I have learned in creating a successful hand-lettering style. I want you to walk away with confidence in your own personal lettering style, and I want to give you the tools and resources to continue practicing. Hand lettering takes time and practice, but you can do it!

More importantly, I hope you are able to use your hand lettering to grow closer to the Lord by memorizing Scripture and meditating on the truths found in His Word. I hope that as you learn how to letter, you are able to worship the Lord with your creativity and give Him thanks for being the ultimate artist and creator.

YOUR GOAL

Let's focus on you. Take a few moments to write out why you're curious to learn more about hand lettering and ideas on how you would like to use your new skills.

SETTING UP YOUR SPACE

This is an exciting time! You've invested in learning the art of hand lettering. After you've gathered your supplies (see the next section for suggestions), I encourage you to set up an inspiring practice area. What makes you feel relaxed? Creating can be extremely therapeutic, so take full advantage of this time to just enjoy learning. When you are ready to start practicing, I encourage you to go to a space where you feel the most inspired. Maybe this is in your studio, your living room, outside at a park, or in a coffee shop. Wherever it is, find that retreat.

Next, have a little fun with it! Set out your lettering tools, make or order your favorite beverage, and put on some of your favorite worship music. Make this a time to enjoy the process.

YOUR TOOLS AND RESOURCES

Before we get started, I want to give you a quick list of supplies I recommend. When I first began hand lettering, I used what I had—Sharpie pens and basic watercolors. These are great to begin with, but over time I've found my absolute favorite tools.

• *Field Notes dot-graph paper notebook.* I love these small notebooks for practicing on the go. They have faint dots on the pages, making it easy to work on your strokes and lay out designs. You'll also want to have a sketchbook or plain paper to use the majority of the time while you're practicing. I use my sketchbook about 98 percent of the time and my nicer paper, like my Arches Cold Pressed Watercolor Pad or my Canson XL Watercolor Textured Paper Pad, when I'm ready to create a piece of artwork.

• *Prismacolor 14420 Ebony Graphite drawing pencil.* I always recommend using pencils when you're first sketching out your design, choosing a layout, and figuring out the best option and style. You don't want to waste precious watercolor or ink. It's important to find a pencil that is smooth and erases well. I love using graphite pencils because they come in various weights, and a lighter weight is easier to erase.

- ***Tombow 62038 Fudenosuke brush pen, soft tip.*** This pen is one of my very favorites because it is really easy to use. When you press down at an angle, you can create different thicknesses of strokes for your letters. The tip holds its shape and glides beautifully while the pen is odorless and precise—amazing for perfecting your letters.

- ***Pentel Arts Aquash water brush pen, light black ink.*** No mess, and it gives you a beautiful watercolor effect. You don't have to constantly dip your pen in ink, and it provides a controlled flow. This pen comes filled with a permanent, acid-free ink, but you can refill it whenever you need with an ink of your choosing. I recommend refilling it with Dr. Ph. Martin's Bombay India Ink that comes with a dropper top so it's easier to fill into the pen. Take it with you wherever you go to keep practicing.

- ***Prismacolor Magic Rub drafting eraser.*** These erasers are wonderful because they not only erase graphite but also erase India ink. No smudging or ripping the paper, either!

PRACTICE

Get familiar with your tools! Take out each tool and practice using it. Get a feel for how the pencils and pens work by making both squiggles and straight lines across a blank sheet of paper.

TIP: *Before using your Pentel brush pen, you will need to unscrew the top, take the red ring off, and then screw the top back on.*

Part One

BASIC HAND LETTERING
AND PRACTICE

LESSON

1

ELEMENTS OF LETTERS

Here are some of the general terms for different parts of letters. Terminology can vary depending on the style of writing. The following descriptions are used primarily in typography, lettering, and calligraphy. It is important to know these definitions so that you can experiment with forms and create beautiful lettering of your own.

* *ascender* — any stroke extending above the waistline

* *ascender line* — an invisible line that capital letters extend to

* *baseline* — an invisible line on which the majority of letters rest

* *bowl* — the curved shape that encloses the round part of a letter

* *counter* — the space within a fully or partially enclosed letter

* *cross stroke* — the horizontal stroke that crosses the letter's stem

* *descender* — the elongated part of a letter that extends below the baseline

* *descender line* — an invisible line that descender letters extend to

* *entrance stroke* — a hairline lead-in stroke with which the letter begins

* *exit stroke* — the hairline stroke with which the letter ends

* *flourish* — curved or decorative elements added to letters or surrounding them that enhance the letter's basic form

* *hairline* — the skinniest stroke found in the letterform

* *ligature* — two or more letters combining to form one character

* *majuscule* — an uppercase letter

* *minuscule* — a lowercase letter

* *overshoot* — the subtle amount to which a rounded letter extends higher than the x-height or lower than the baseline

* *shoulder* — the connecting stroke (often curved) that extends from the stem

* *stem* — the primary vertical stroke within the letter

* *swash* — similar to the flourish, the exaggerated added decorative element extending to the left or right of the first and last letter of a word

* *terminal* — either end of any stroke— straight, diagonal, or curved

* *waistline* — the invisible line running across the top of lowercase letters (also called the median)

* *weight* — the amount of thickness and size of a letter

* *x-height* — the amount of space between the waistline and baseline

Stem

Stroke Shoulder Bowl

Ascender Line

Ascender Height

Waistline

X-Height

Baseline

Descender Height

Descender Line

Anatomy

Counter

Exit Stroke

Entrance Stroke

Hairline

Swash

Ascender

Ligature

Tittle

of lettering

Flourish

Overshoot

Descender

LESSON

2

BASIC STROKES

Before we get started, let's take a look at a couple major things that can affect your lettering outcome. The first is the way you hold your pen. You want to hold your pen loosely and a little bit to the side—not vertically or with a tight grip, which would wear out the tip of your pen faster and produce poor lettering results.

The second thing I want to mention is practice. You don't have to have great handwriting to become great at lettering. All you need is to commit to practicing so that you develop the muscle memory to create consistent, smooth lettering. If you practice enough, you will learn exactly how much pressure and speed to apply to make your own beautiful lettering.

The key to the basic strokes of hand lettering is the thickness of your strokes. When you move the pen upward, the strokes should be thin. And when you move the pen downward, the strokes should be thick. Thin going up, thick going down.

In order to create the thin and thick strokes, you need to hold your brush at about a 45-degree angle and apply pressure to the pen to achieve the thick stroke going down and light pressure to create a thin, delicate line going up. When you are moving your pen, your whole arm should be moving, not just your wrist. Take your time practicing these techniques before moving on.

Use your brush pen to form downstrokes in the space provided. Remember to apply pressure to the pen to achieve the thick stroke.

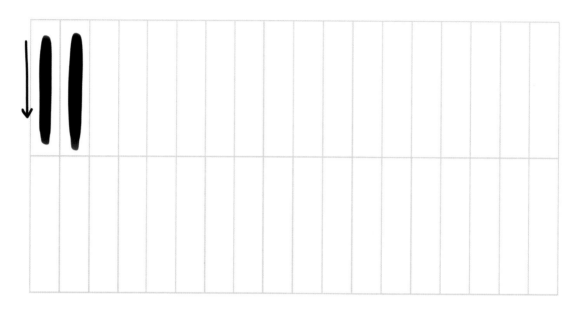

Now practice your upstrokes following the example below. You want to use light pressure to create a thin, delicate line.

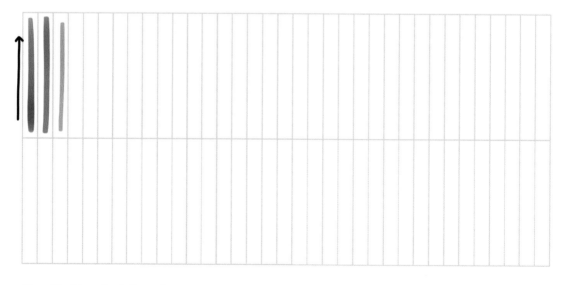

To create cross strokes, you'll want to apply medium pressure as I've done below.

Putting your upstrokes and downstrokes together, you are going to create loops, waves, and curves to help solidify your understanding of how pressure affects your strokes. Copy the patterns below on the lines provided.

LESSON

3

BASIC STROKES THAT FORM LETTERS

Mastering the basic techniques will make you a better hand letterer. This foundation of brush strokes will help you on your journey to developing your own style and becoming a better artist. You must be able to deconstruct the letter in order to understand how to build it.

Practice the basic strokes listed below with both your brush pen and felt-tip pens.

Entrance and Exit Strokes

Underturn Stroke

Overturn Stroke

Compound Curve

Oval

Ascending and Descending Loops

LESSON

4

PRACTICING YOUR LETTERS

See if you can identify the basic strokes within each letter. You know what the letters of the alphabet are supposed to look like. However, what makes script letters stand out are their contrasting thick and thin lines and where they should be applied—so you have to follow some rules. It will make your life much easier if you follow the correct order and apply the basic strokes with the correct directional pressure.

TIPS AND TRICKS

Try forming your letters by piecing each basic stroke together to make a completed letter. After each stroke, lift your pen and apply the next stroke. This allows you to take your time and really think about the direction you're supposed to follow and the pressure you're supposed to apply to make sure your letters look their best. After you have mastered the first method, try to keep your pen in contact with the paper between each stroke transition, creating one continuous flow.

Practice your letters. Continue practicing each of the individual letters in a separate notebook if needed. Feel free to explore different styles and add extra elements to your letters. In later chapters, we will be focusing on each letter of the alphabet in depth.

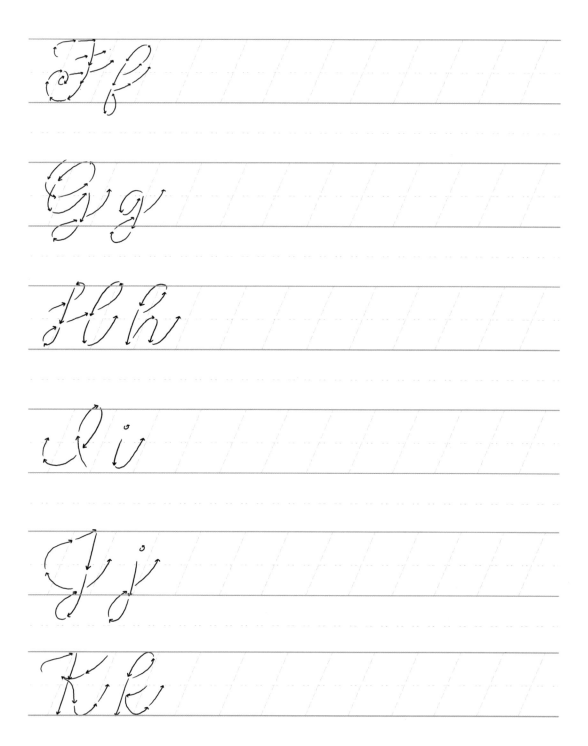

L l

M m

N n

O o

P p

Q q

Rr Rr

Ss Ss

Tt Tt

Uu Uu

Vv Vv

Ww Ww

Xx

Yy

Zz

LESSON 5

ADDING FLOURISHES

Flourishes may or may not be a part of your style, but before you rule them out, let's take some time to play around with them. Flourishes don't have to be twirling and swirling; they can be simple, straight, or bold. I've found that it helps to try and keep your flourishes flowing in a similar direction or angle as one another so that they maintain balance within your piece. Flourishes are a great way to fill in needed space or add extra flair to your lettering. They can be so much fun and add a lot of personality to your work.

decorative

SANDWICH

ORNATE

framed

FLOURISHES

First, let's start by practicing some simple flourish designs. Practice each flourish in the space provided next to it.

DECORATIVE ELEMENTS

There are several different ways to add decorative elements to your flourishes. Here are some examples. Use different pens to try your hand at some of these techniques.

ADVANCED FLOURISHES

If you want to be a little more challenged, you can practice some of these advanced flourishes. Try each one and add your own unique touch if you want.

Combining some of these different elements to create a completed design is a great strategy. Pick one or two elements to create a completed flourish. If you make your flourish bold, try making your lettering simple. If you make your flourish small, try making your lettering large. Using contrasts like this can help you create an interesting piece.

CREATING A COMPLETE PIECE

To practice knowing where to apply flourishes in your design, start by writing out the word very simply on a blank piece of paper. Notice where the ascenders, descenders, and ligatures are in your word. For example, if you have any ascenders or descenders with loops, those might be good places to add flourishes. If you have any t's, you could add a beautiful crossbar flourish.

Next, decide which elements you want to exaggerate with a flourish. Beside the word, sketch out some flourish ideas, referring to the examples I shared above.

Decide if you want to add just a few decorative elements, frame the entire piece with flourishes, or allow the flourishes to take center stage in an ornate composition. Once you've decided on a design, sketch it out completely. After you've sketched it out, you can decide what weight you want to give your flourishes and lettering and what extra elements you might want to add to complete your design.

LESSON 6

LAYING OUT YOUR LETTERING

We've been working on a lot of technique, and now we are going to start the process of putting everything together. If you find yourself struggling to create a completed piece of lettering, follow these steps to assist you in laying out your word or phrase.

1. MAKE A FEW SKETCHES

Loosely sketch out some variations of a design in pencil. Don't worry about making them perfect; just get your ideas down on paper.

TIP: *Choose a shape as a loose guideline.*

Picking a square, circle, banner, or other shape for your letters to fit into can help you create a more visually appealing piece. People are attracted to artwork that looks good from a distance, so the shape of your piece will attract people even before they read it.

TIP: *Draw the standout words first.*

Are there certain words in your layout that need to stand out more than others? Draw those first, and then add the other text around it. This ensures that the standout word(s) really pop and make a statement.

2. PICK THE WINNER

After choosing the best design, sketch it again in pencil. Take time to consider how the words are going to fill the composition. Look for opportunities to add flourishes and ornamental elements to your design.

TIP: *Wait to add your flourishes until after you've finished laying out your lettering.*

Adding the flourishes last gives you a chance to fill open spaces, choose where the flourishes will extend, and make a more balanced piece. If you've chosen standout words, you can add flourishes to those first before finishing your piece if you want.

3. ADD WEIGHT TO YOUR LETTERS

Go over your sketch again, adding weight to your letters, making them thicker on the downstrokes. Adjust the spacing and flourishes as needed.

4. FINALIZE WITH A PEN

Using your brush or ink pen, finalize your drawing. This is where the small nylon tip of your pen comes in handy for making everything look crisp and precise.

TIP: *Use tracing paper.*

If you're really struggling with laying out your lettering, draw your words individually on tracing paper. Then cut out the words and practice arranging them. This will help you see where you need to make edits, change the sizing, extend letters, or add more spacing.

7

DEVELOPING YOUR STYLE

Developing your style may take time, and you may only begin to discover it today. But with practice, you will narrow it down and fine-tune it. Creating a personal style you love will allow you to have a consistent base to go back to as you work. Over time, you may develop several different styles that you can use for different projects.

When you're trying to figure out your style, it's important to take in a lot of creative inspiration. The key is not to copy another artist's work. I recommend filling up an inspiration board full of images that inspire you—either from Pinterest or by printing out images and creating a physical one—but when you're ready to sit down and practice or create something for yourself or your business, don't have those images right in front of you. Use them as inspiration in the back of your mind. Not only will having them right in front of you hinder your own creative process, but you'll also be more likely to copy them.

What kind of lettering are you drawn to? Is there a common theme among the images on your inspiration board? Write down some thoughts about what inspires you and what you'd like to apply to your own lettering style.

Then practice writing how you'd like each of your letters to look. Is your lettering loose and free flowing or tighter and more controlled? After playing around with your name and various words, write out your thoughts about the exercise. Circle your favorite styles and note what you want to improve.

high & low   *elegant*

bouncy   *curly*

freehand   *BOLD*

Romantic   *Whispy*

LETTER ADJUSTMENTS

There are many ways to write each letter of the alphabet in calligraphy. Sometimes it helps to look at the different ways you could adjust each letter to create an alternate form. Take a look at these alternate examples to give you some ideas for developing your own style.

ADJUST THE OVERSHOOT

The overshoot is the amount to which a letter extends higher than the x-height or lower than the baseline. Try going above or below those lines as in the examples shown.

ADJUST THE ANGLE

Although the angle at which you write your letters should stay consistent within each piece of artwork, it can be fun to play around with different angles to create different looks. Just be sure to keep the angle consistent throughout your piece.

ADJUST THE LOOP SIZE

One of the most fun ways, in my opinion, to create alternate characters is to adjust the size of the ascending or descending loops on different letters to be more or less exaggerated.

ADJUST THE FLOURISHES

Flourishes speak a lot about the style of a piece of hand lettering. They can add elegance or create a whimsical feel, depending on how you use them and how ornate you create them to be.

ADJUST THE LIGATURES

Adding ligatures to your piece makes it incredibly unique and truly hand done. Ligatures are two or more characters combining to create one letterform, so try using different techniques to combine letters within your piece.

Ultimately, the most important thing is to keep each piece consistent within itself. So, once you decide what style to use, stick to that style within each piece of artwork. Sometimes it's appropriate to use more than one style within a piece, but if you do, I would recommend using no more than two and to be careful to balance them within the piece.

After you narrow down what you want your main style to look like, letter the complete alphabet using that style. Later, you can use this as a reference for that style as you work. Over time, you may create alphabets in other styles that you can reference. You can use the following alternate letter examples for inspiration to help you develop your own.

Please note that I'm not trying to limit your creativity by having you stick to one style. You can, of course, change the way you write your letters every time you create something if you wish. And when you add in flourishes or decorative elements, you may want to change them each time too. The intention of this lesson is to get you to home in on a specific way of lettering that is your "go-to." Soon you will have multiple styles in your tool belt to use.

Just like any other skill, lettering takes time, practice, and dedication. You might not arrive at something you are completely happy with right away, but give yourself a little grace and keep practicing! It takes work. For me, it took nearly a year of practice to develop my unique style and start selling my prints. It might take you a while to discover your style too.

A A A A a a a

B B B B L L L b b

C C C C c c c

D D D D D d d d

E E E E e e e

F F F f f f f

G G G g g g

H H h h h h

I I I i i i

J J J j j j

K K K k k k

L L L L l l

Hand Lettering God's Word

$SSSSSssss$

$LLLLtttt$

$UUUUu$

$VVV vvv$

$WWWWW$

XXx

Yy Yy Yy Gy y y by y

Zz Zz

Part Two

A-TO-Z LETTER PRACTICE
AND DEVOTIONS

LETTER PRACTICE

In the chapters that follow, we will focus on each letter of the alphabet so you can practice them one at a time. Please continue to go back and practice previous lessons as needed. Along with each letter, I have chosen a corresponding verse or passage of Scripture for you to practice lettering as well as memorizing. The challenge of lettering a larger piece will be a fun way to put together all you have learned. I hope you are able to take these chapters slowly and be filled with peace as you meditate on God's Word in a creative way. As you write out the verses, I pray that God will transform your heart and mind.

1. Create space in your day and surroundings to meditate on God's Word.

2. Take time to soak in the Word and pray.

3. Practice a different letter each day, keeping in mind what you learned in previous lessons.

4. Practice memorizing Scripture and putting together all your learned skills as you letter each verse.

CHALLENGE

Practice lettering each Scripture several times and pick your favorite. Place the lettered verse where you can see it and continue to meditate on God's Word throughout your day.

I PRAY THAT OUT OF

his glorious riches he may strengthen you with power

THROUGH HIS SPIRIT IN YOUR INNER BEING, SO THAT

Christ may dwell in your hearts through faith

AND I PRAY THAT YOU, BEING ROOTED AND ESTABLISHED IN LOVE,
MAY HAVE POWER, TOGETHER WITH ALL THE LORD'S HOLY PEOPLE,

to grasp how wide and long and high and deep is the love of Christ and to know this love that surpasses

KNOWLEDGE - THAT YOU MAY BE FILLED TO THE MEASURE OF ALL THE

fullness of God.
Ephesians 3:16-19

As for me and my house, we will serve the LORD.

JOSHUA 24:15 ESV

We can often find ourselves hiding parts of our lives from the Lord, allowing Him free reign in every area of our hearts except a few rooms that we keep to ourselves. We might think, *It's okay; I gave Him all those rooms. He doesn't need to see this one.* But the Lord asks us to give over our whole heart to Him—and that means every part of it. We cannot live in two worlds, serving both God and our sinful desires. We must choose whom we will serve.

Lord, thank You for Your cleansing presence in my life. I ask that You would give me the strength to surrender to You. To give over not only my sinful desires, but also my sense of control over the blessings in my life. That I would find peace in knowing that You are Lord over everything.

—————————————— **REFLECTION** ——————————————

What areas of your heart are you hiding from God? Do you have hidden sin you have yet to give over to Him? Spend some time in prayer, asking God to open your eyes and heart in order to know Him more and to serve Him in every area of your life.

A a A a A a A a

As for Me
AND
my house
we will
serve
THE
Lord
Joshua 24 15

Be strong and courageous! Do not be afraid or discouraged.
For the LORD your God is with you wherever you go.

JOSHUA 1:9 NLT

Have you fallen into the trap of secluding God to a specific time and place? Like He belongs in this box you've labeled "quiet time," and if you can't find a space or moment to open that box in complete silence, then the box has to be put away until you can find that moment? The reality is, God is with us wherever we go! He isn't just there when we are reading Scripture and studying His Word. He is with us while we wash the dishes, while we spend time with a friend, when we are at work, when we rest, and when we drive home. He is with us in the most extraordinary and the most mundane of tasks. What a wonderful and peace-giving truth.

My true comforter! My restorer! My healer! You are with me always. You give me freedom from anxiety and feeling weak, and You show me I am capable through Your strength. Sometimes I forget about Your omnipresence and the power this reality has over my life. Lord, help me stay rooted in Your presence.

REFLECTION

What would it look like for you to stay in touch with God's presence throughout your entire day? Are there places in your life where you are allowing fear to have control? I encourage you to submit those fears to God—lay them at the feet of the One who can be your strength and courage through any situation.

Be strong and courageous
do not be afraid
or discouraged
for the Lord your
God is with you
wherever you
go

Joshua 1:9

Cast all your anxiety on him because he cares for you.

1 PETER 5:7

Our good Father created this beautiful world. Due to man's fall and our sinful nature, pain and suffering are unavoidable. Just by existing, we are broken and in need of restoration. And living in an imperfect world has its share of consequences. There are moments in our life when we feel truly brokenhearted, isolated, and alone. We feel weary, burdened, and overwhelmed. But God is worthy of our trust and able to hold our broken hearts.

Lord, I cast all my anxiety and fear and brokenness on You. You are for me and not against me. You do not withhold; You are good and have given me purpose. You know exactly what I truly need. You aren't a taker—You are a giver. You cast my fears aside with perfect love. You fill the empty space in my heart and give me strength.

REFLECTION

Spend some time meditating on the following verses. As you read through each one, write down what these verses say about God's character. Why should we not be afraid?

God has not given us a spirit of fear and timidity, but of power, love, and self-discipline (2 Timothy 1:7 NLT).

Do not fear, for I am with you; do not be dismayed, for I am your God. I will strengthen you and help you; I will uphold you with my righteous right hand...For I am the LORD your God who takes hold of your right hand and says to you, Do not fear; I will help you (Isaiah 41:10,13).

$\mathcal{C}c$ $\mathcal{C}c$ $\mathcal{C}c$ $\mathcal{C}c$ $\mathcal{C}c$

Cast all your anxiety on him because he cares for you

1 PETER 5:7

*Do nothing out of selfish ambition or vain conceit. Rather,
in humility value others above yourselves.*

PHILIPPIANS 2:3

Shortly after Drew and I had our firstborn, Drew lost his job. I was just coming out of my first round of postpartum depression, and we had bills to pay, a mortgage to cover, and a new baby to take care of. After going through our emergency savings in the first couple months, we didn't know what we were going to do. We were feeling hopeless, tired, and in need.

At one point, Drew broke down and told his community of guy friends about the burden we were carrying. A few weeks later, the guys handed Drew an envelope filled with enough money to cover two months of our mortgage payment. Drew opened the envelope, and his eyes immediately welled up with tears. We were overcome with gratitude and truly humbled. It still makes me emotional when I think of the picture of selfless love our community displayed.

When we stop thinking about ourselves so much and instead consider the people in our lives—thinking about what it means to make their lives better and to show them the love of Christ—we begin to value others more than ourselves. We begin to find joy in giving our time, our money, our resources, and ourselves.

Lord, mold my heart so that I desire to love and serve others. I pray that You would grant me discernment to know and listen for the needs of others so that I can serve and bless the people around me.

--- **REFLECTION** ---

Make a list of the people closest to you and write down two or three ways you could show the love of Christ to them. This doesn't always look like giving monetarily. It could be as simple as making them a cup of coffee, praying with them, serving them, or sitting down and really listening to their heart.

Dd Dd Dd

Do nothing out of selfish ambition or vain conceit. Rather, in humility value others above yourselves.

PHILIPPIANS 2:3

Each of you should give what you have decided in your heart to give, not reluctantly or under compulsion, for God loves a cheerful giver.

2 CORINTHIANS 9:7

Sometimes we are afraid or reluctant to give, unless the act is accompanied by the hope of getting. We wonder, *If I give this much, how much of my investment will be returned to me?* We are eager to hold on to what we have because we are afraid of being left empty. It can be easy to forget that our salvation doesn't come from our possessions or talents.

True giving expects nothing in return. It manifests out of being so secure in the hope of having everything we need in Christ—which no one can take away—that we are free to give joyfully. "This hope is a strong and trustworthy anchor for our souls" (Hebrews 6:19 NLT).

God doesn't want us to give because we feel we have to; His desire is for us to find joy in giving. He knows that we will find more lasting joy from giving than receiving. "It is more blessed to give than to receive" (Acts 20:35).

Thank You, Lord, for the gift of Your Son, Jesus Christ. You have set an example for me of what it means to give graciously. Help me be so secure in the hope I have in You that I am able to give without reluctance. Open my heart and hands so that I may be a vessel for You.

REFLECTION

What does it look like for you to be a cheerful giver? What has God entrusted you with that you could offer? Are you so attached to the things you have (possessions, talents, gifts, money, etc.) that you wouldn't be willing to give them away if God asked?

Each of you should give what you have decided in your heart to give, not reluctantly or under compulsion, for God loves a cheerful giver.

2 Corinthians 9:7

"For I know the plans I have for you," declares the LORD, "plans to prosper you and not to harm you, plans to give you hope and a future."

JEREMIAH 29:11

How many times have you realized that your inner dialogue includes more negative words than positive ones? If we aren't carefully guarding our thoughts, it's easy to allow a grim narrative to take root in our minds and—eventually—our hearts. This has the potential to make us pessimistic about our future and also spawns the kind of lies the enemy wants us to succumb to: I can't do it; I am not enough; I will fail.

The words and thoughts we allow to rule over our lives become the truths we believe. If we tell ourselves how bad we have it, we can start to believe that our lives are lacking or afflicted. Maybe that seems exaggerated to you, but think about it: What thoughts have you been speaking over your circumstances recently? When we focus on the wound, sometimes we miss the beauty and opportunities for gratitude in front of us.

Lord, I know You are good. When I become bitter or self-focused, help me redirect my thoughts to You. You promise that if I trust in You and not on my own understanding that You will direct my path. Direct my thoughts, Lord. Show me glimpses of Your presence and where You are working in my life.

—————————————— **REFLECTION** ——————————————

I challenge you to rewrite the narrative that goes on between your ears. Look closely at what God says about you, your life, and His plans for you in His Word. Obstacles, difficulties, and sadness can define your life in one of two ways: 1) They can make you feel like a victim, or 2) they can turn you toward faith and hope in a good God who desires hope for you. Can you find the thread of grace and goodness He has placed within the tapestry of your circumstances? Can you see an opportunity to give Him glory in your life—where you are right now?

For I know the plans I have for you, declares the Lord. Plans to prosper you and not to harm you, plans to give you hope and a future. Jeremiah 29:11

Greater love has no one than this: to lay down one's life for one's friends.

JOHN 15:13

What is community? Community is more than just a group of people—it is a sense of fellowship we have from doing life together, from bearing one another's burdens and sharing our resources and hearts. In our youth, friendships can be easy to find through school, work, sports, and other activities. As we grow older, though, community can be more difficult to cultivate.

After college, I moved to a new city and was not connected anywhere. I felt isolated and realized that I had spent most of my life with community all around me. Community that I did not create, but that was created for me. It had been a beautiful blessing, but because of that, I thought community would just "happen" naturally wherever I went.

You cannot expect community to just come to you. You have to make time for it. You have to be willing to go somewhere new, talk to people you don't know, and put in the hard work of pouring out your heart into others' lives. Community is vital for us to flourish—we are not meant to do life alone. Challenge yourself to stop waiting for people to come to you and instead seek them.

Father, I want to be in community with others. I pray that You would help me be brave as I seek out other people in order to form deep relationships. Being vulnerable is difficult, but You have promised to give me strength and courage when I need it.

REFLECTION

Here are some ideas for creating community:

- going to church groups, Bible studies, and events
- finding hobbies you have in common with someone you meet and inviting them to join you in an event that complements your shared interest (such as hiking, painting, or gardening)
- working as a volunteer
- creating weekly movie nights or outings for current acquaintances

Greater love has no one than this: to lay down one's life for one's friends

John 15:13

He will wipe away every tear from their eyes, and death shall be no more, neither shall there be mourning, nor crying, nor pain anymore, for the former things have passed away.

REVELATION 21:4 ESV

Oh, how our souls crave this truth! No more tears or death or sorrow. Everything new and as God intended it to be. Sometimes being earthbound with heaven in mind can feel unavailing. Like we want to skip to the end of the book to get to the part where restoration has been found. What is the purpose of embracing this life amid pain and sadness if we have the promise of a perfect future in communion with Christ?

God did not intend for us to wait until heaven to start the process of restoration. Scripture says in 2 Corinthians 5:17 that "if anyone is in Christ, he is a new creation. The old has passed away; behold, the new has come" (ESV). This means if we believe in Christ, our souls have been restored. And we are free to live the most radical life of love and sacrifice here on earth. We then should live in such a way that makes people look at our lives and wonder why we are filled with such hope. Because we know the ending of the book already—we know that no matter how much conflict and suffering and evil we see around us, God is going to make all things new (Revelation 21:5).

Lord, everything in me longs for heaven. Help me live in such a way here on earth that I point people toward You. Thank You for the glorious gift of hope You have given us—that no matter what sadness we encounter, we can face it because of the certainty we have in Christ.

--- **REFLECTION** ---

What does it look like to live a life of love and sacrifice? Does hope spill out from you in such a way that others notice something different about you? How can you point others to Christ in your everyday life?

He will wipe away
every tear from their
eyes, and death shall
be no more, neither
shall there be
mourning nor
crying nor pain
anymore, for the
former things have
passed away.
Revelation 21:4

I know what it is to be in need, and I know what it is to have plenty. I have learned the secret of being content in any and every situation, whether well fed or hungry, whether living in plenty or in want. I can do all this through him who gives me strength.

PHILIPPIANS 4:12-13

We all encounter times of waiting in our lives. Times when we feel like the present will never end. It is easy to become anxious and demanding. But God has asked us to wait with patience and to be content in our current circumstance. Our journey is not just about the beginning and the end. It is also about the middle. The waiting part is important, as is whether or not you wait well. Because the outcome of what you are waiting for is not guaranteed.

In our human minds, inconvenience is the enemy. Being "put out" is what we avoid, and glory for ourselves is what we seek. Sometimes at all costs. But God asks us to be content in any situation. First, that means we have to be willing to be placed in any situation. We have to be open to God's desire for our lives. And second, we have to find contentment wherever He has placed us, knowing that His purpose is greater than our longing for what's convenient.

God, You know best. I pray that I would surrender control to You and Your timeline instead of insisting we follow mine. Instead of my life playing out as I have planned in my mind, I pray that I would be in the center of Your will for my life.

REFLECTION

Surrendering control to God and practicing gratitude are two ways to become content in your circumstances. What are some ways you can practice gratitude in your daily life?

$\mathcal{U}i$ $\mathcal{U}i$ $\mathcal{U}i$

I can do all this through him who gives me strength

philippians 4:13

Judge not, that you be not judged. For with the judgment you pronounce you will be judged, and with the measure you use it will be measured to you.

MATTHEW 7:1-2 ESV

Not sure about you, but I believe I would make a great judge. I watch all sorts of scenarios on TV, social media, YouTube, and other places that trick me into believing I am qualified to make judgments on someone I have never met. Somewhere deep down, we tend to believe we would do better than others, or we define others by a single mishap.

Making snap judgments has many problems though. One of which is that it cuts out grace completely—and we all need grace. Our judging nature makes it easy for us to write off another person as "beyond repair" or "not worth praying for" if we choose not to look at them with grace and love. And doesn't that mean we are saying God isn't big enough or His compassion isn't great enough to reach them? All of God's children are worth waiting for, praying for, and hoping for.

Lord, You are the only source of real affirmation. When I have feelings of pride or inferiority, help me look to You for affirmation instead of lashing out at others. Your unconditional love and grace cover me and make me feel secure. Forgive me for not believing You are capable of restoring anyone and anything.

REFLECTION

Who in your life do you consider a "lost cause"—maybe not worth your prayers or efforts? Grace is a great leveler—we all need it, all the time. Not one of us has done anything to deserve God's salvation, but He is so good. He offers us all salvation through His Son, Jesus Christ. Prayer is a great way to soften your heart. Consider dedicating time to pray for the people in your life who need more love and grace.

Judge not that you be not judged. For with the judgment you pronounce you will be judged, and with the measure you use it will be measured to you.

Matthew 7:1-2

Keep loving one another earnestly, since love covers a multitude of sins.

1 PETER 4:8 ESV

I used to always think of myself as a hard worker, someone who had something good to bring to the table. I was confident in my abilities and in what God's purpose was for my life. Fast-forward to a few years ago—I had become a mother for the first time. I felt purposeful in my call to motherhood; however, I realized I was not accomplishing some of my other goals as quickly as I had hoped.

With the birth of each new child, I felt extreme purpose in what I was doing with my children, but also extreme panic because I felt I was losing my place in other areas of life. At times it seemed motherhood completely defined me. Because of this, I was envious of others who were using their gifts and abilities. Every time someone accomplished something great, I panicked a little. Everyone else was moving forward in their life, doing great things. Meanwhile, I seemed to be frozen in place.

But our place at the table is not dictated by others. We all have a divine purpose for which we were each created. Celebrating others never takes away from the calling God has put on your life. Your dreams and ambitions are still part of you. There will be a time for them, even if it isn't today. Keep pressing forward in what God has called you to right now. Focus your heart on doing it well. We all carry a promise of purpose in glorifying Christ. Hold fast to the confidence that God has called you and you are loved.

I am so often tempted to compare myself to others, Lord. But You have given me a unique calling and purpose. Make me aware of Your purpose for my life and help me stay focused on it. When I am tempted to look around, draw me back to the fullness of Your presence.

REFLECTION

We all have an area of our life where we feel inadequate. What does that look like for you? How can you celebrate others in their unique gifts?

Keep loving one another earnestly, since love covers a multitude of sins.

1 PETER 4:8

Let us think of ways to motivate one another to acts of love and good works.

HEBREWS 10:24 NLT

We live in a self-focused world. It's easy to believe the lie that everything is about me when it is subtly shown to us wherever we look. Sometimes we forget that this is God's story, and that part of our purpose is to motivate one another toward Christ. Second Corinthians 3:18 says, "We all, who with unveiled faces contemplate the Lord's glory, are being transformed into his image with ever-increasing glory, which comes from the Lord, who is the Spirit." This transformation is not something we do in isolation, but together.

Are you going about your day so focused on yourself that you forget about the people around you? Do you think of thoughtful ways to uplift your spouse and show them you are there for them? When you go into church, are you so focused on what you are going to get out of your time there that you forget to ask what you might be able to give—not just to God, but in service to the other people around you? Are we too tired, too busy, too overwhelmed to turn our focus toward others and pour out encouragement and love?

Thank You, Lord, for Your Holy Spirit, who is here to console and strengthen us. I want to be an encouragement to the people around me. I know spending more time with You, God, will fill my cup and give me the capacity to pour into others. Give me the desire to seek You more.

REFLECTION

Are there people in your life who sharpen you and push you toward Christ? Challenge yourself to be that friend to others. Do you need encouragement? Who can come alongside and pray for God's redeeming work in your life? Would you be bold enough to walk that road with someone else as well?

Let us think of ways to motivate one another to acts of love and good works.
Hebrews 10:24

My grace is sufficient for you, for my power is made perfect in weakness.

2 CORINTHIANS 12:9

We all have experienced some sort of darkness or trial in our lives. Maybe you are still experiencing it. Most recently for me, this darkness was postpartum depression. It was consuming, and there were moments that were so foggy and dark that I could not see past the overwhelming despair. I would cry out to God about feeling trapped in this sadness, but I was so hesitant to ask Him to heal me of it. I was afraid of being disappointed if He said no. What if I was to bear this burden—what then? How could I endure this? And how on earth could I find contentment in the midst of this depression?

My grace is sufficient for you.

I felt God speak to me and say, "What if I have decided that this is your story? Am I still good?" And I immediately responded, "Yes, You are still good."

Through prayer and time, the Lord has given me peace in this season. He can do that for you too.

We keep asking God for healing and restoration, all the while praising Him for His goodness. We seek contentment even if He decides to leave us with this thorn—having faith that His grace and presence will be enough for us. He has given us His Spirit to comfort us, console us, strengthen us, and make us brave. So we are able to face uncertainty with courage. Not because we are not scared, but because we are afraid and lean into faith despite it all.

Lord, it's not through my achievements that You will be known, but You will be glorified despite any area in which I am lacking. You can do all things. You do not need me to be strong on my own; rather, You delight in showing Your power through my weaknesses. Lord, thank You for Your grace that covers every deficiency.

REFLECTION

Is there a burden or darkness that you are bearing right now? Boldly ask the Lord to take it away, but also pray that He would give you grace to find peace and contentment even in the midst of it.

Mm Mm Mm Mm

my grace is sufficient for you for my power is made perfect in weakness

2 Corinthians 12:9

*Now may the Lord of peace himself give you peace at
all times in every way. The Lord be with you all.*

2 THESSALONIANS 3:16 ESV

When too many things fight for our attention, they can leave us feeling completely spent. So we buy stuff we think will make us happier. We work out more, plan vacations, clean out our closets, hustle harder, and pamper ourselves. We deceive ourselves into thinking these things will bring us the peace and purpose we desperately desire.

But the only way to find true peace and purpose is by resting our souls in Jesus. Ephesians 2:14 tells us, "He himself is our peace." We desperately need to center our fight for peace around the only One who gives it: Christ. We can do this by spending time in Scripture, claiming the truths of His Word, getting on our knees and praying, and seeking intimacy with Him. God will not scream for our attention the way other things in our lives do. The enemy of our soul wants to do everything to distract us from looking to Christ. The enemy is fine with us doing good things as long as they distract us from the best thing—Jesus Himself.

Philippians 4:6-7 says, "Present your requests to God. And the peace of God, which transcends all understanding, will guard your hearts and your minds in Christ Jesus." Thank You, Lord, for Your peace that guards my heart and mind and never leaves me. Help me notice what's going on around me instead of being distracted. Make me present. Remind me that true peace and purpose are found in You alone.

REFLECTION

Take note of everything in your life that falsely promises to bring you peace and contentment. When you are tired and overwhelmed, what are you most likely to turn to instead of God? Knowing this, you can recognize the distraction more clearly when it comes and redirect your search for peace to the only One who gives true peace—the Lord.

$\mathcal{N}\,n\quad\mathcal{N}\,n\quad\mathcal{N}\,n$

Now may
the Lord of
peace himself
give you
peace at all
times in
every way

2 THESS. 3:16

Our God whom we serve is able to deliver us from the burning fiery furnace, and he will deliver us out of your hand, O king. But if not, be it known to you, O king, that we will not serve your gods or worship the golden image that you have set up.

DANIEL 3:17-18 ESV

The situation looks hopeless, and we pray God will save us. But if not, He is still good.

As Shadrach, Meshach, and Abednego were thrown into the fiery furnace of King Nebuchadnezzar, I am sure they were prepared to die. They knew God was powerful enough to save them—greater than any king or army. But God doesn't promise to save us from the threats of this world. He has promised to walk with us and give us His peace—knowing that He will be glorified whether we are rescued from our circumstances or not. Shadrach, Meshach, and Abednego boldly proclaimed God's power and goodness without knowing if He would save them.

In 2 Corinthians 1:10, Paul says, "He who rescued us from so deadly a peril will continue to rescue us; on him we have set our hope that he will rescue us again" (NRSV). This hope we have that God will rescue us is a belief that He is capable of walking into our situation and changing it. He may not rescue us from our situation here on earth, but in the end, if we know Him, He is going to rescue us from death and into heaven.

Lord, help me in long, hard days of quiet faithfulness as I endure the various trials before me. Help me hold out my hands and accept Your will in these situations instead of trying to bend Your will to meet mine. I know You are powerful enough to rescue me, but if You choose not to, help me speak the truth that You are still good. Because it is for Your greater good that You allow me to endure.

REFLECTION

How do you deal with being disappointed when God doesn't act in the way you think He should? I encourage you to practice getting on your knees when you pray and opening your hands. These physical actions remind us that He is Lord and worthy of our praise.

Oo *Oo* *Oo*

Our God whom we serve is able to deliver us from the burning fiery furnace, and he will deliver us out of your hand, O king. But if not, be it known to you, O king, that we will not serve your gods or worship the golden image that you have set up.

Daniel 3:17-18

Put on then, as God's chosen ones, holy and beloved, compassionate hearts, kindness, humility, meekness, and patience, bearing with one another and, if one has a complaint against another, forgiving each other; as the Lord has forgiven you, so you also must forgive.

COLOSSIANS 3:12-13 ESV

When I was very young, my biological dad left our family. For years, I focused on how God had redeemed our lives through my wonderful stepdad, Kevin. God had given us someone in our lives who loved and cared for us. But years later, I realized that even though I was so grateful to God for what He had done to restore our lives, I had never really forgiven my biological dad. I had skipped right over that part, hoping it would just go away.

You may also be someone who skips over forgiveness because it doesn't fix the past or because you just want to move on. But the point of forgiveness is not to alter the past, but to show the same grace to others that God has shown to you. Forgiveness frees up your heart from resentment and anger. It allows you to be compassionate toward others and see yourself as equally undeserving of God's grace. "All have sinned and fall short of the glory of God, and all are justified freely by his grace through the redemption that came by Christ Jesus" (Romans 3:23-24). Christ portrayed the ultimate picture of grace, forgiveness, and love by dying for our sins and blanketing us in His forgiveness.

Lord, I am undeserving of Your grace and forgiveness. Thank You for sending Your Son, Jesus Christ, to die so that I might live. As Ephesians 2:8 says, "It is by grace you have been saved, through faith—and this is not from yourselves, it is the gift of God." Help me be compassionate toward others. Soften my heart, Lord, that I might forgive as You forgave me.

REFLECTION

Are there people in your life from whom you have withheld forgiveness? I encourage you to write down the reasons why and then pray that the Lord would soften your heart. He cares about what hurts you, but He also knows that unforgiveness can create a barrier between you and Him.

Put on then, as God's chosen ones, holy and beloved, compassionate hearts, kindness, humility, meekness, and patience, bearing with one another and, if one has a complaint against another, forgiving each other; as the Lord has forgiven you, so you also must forgive.

Colossians 3:12-13

In quietness and confidence is your strength.

ISAIAH 30:15 NLT

Drew and I went through a time recently where we were forced to change a lot of things at once. We had to sell our house and many of our possessions and move an hour away into a small basement apartment. While many blessings and silver linings were in this situation, it was still difficult to process all the changes that had to happen. At first, I tried to just focus on having a positive outlook. That was definitely helpful, but I never addressed my feelings of loss and sadness, so they lingered in the background.

It's wonderful to have a positive perspective on life, but it's equally important to come to that positive place alongside working through the negative. Instead of shutting out those feelings, I needed to say them out loud—bringing them into the light. Then I could filter them through God's truth and a positive perspective—one that is focused on heaven and the bigger picture God has for our lives.

Thank You, Lord, for Your truth and the promise of redemption You have given me. When changes happen, help me sit still and bring my concerns to You first. As I process my emotions, You are there with me. You are my comforter, "for the LORD comforts his people and will have compassion on his afflicted ones," as Isaiah 49:13 says.

REFLECTION

What kind of loss or change have you experienced recently? Sit quietly for a while and allow yourself to think through your emotions. Write down what you are feeling and tell the Lord what you wrote. Have a conversation with Him about why you feel that way. Then start working on developing a positive perspective that includes the hope of heaven.

IN
Quietness
AND
confidence
is your
Strength

ISAIAH 30:15

Rejoice always, pray without ceasing, give thanks in all circumstances;
for this is the will of God in Christ Jesus for you.

1 THESSALONIANS 5:16-18 ESV

Teaching children to say "thank you" can be a constant test of patience. No matter how many times they are reminded, it seems we humans are born having to learn gratefulness. It has to be trained within us. We are all born into this world in sin, with a constant need for refinement. Saying "thank you" in the moment when we are given something—even a good gift—has to be formed into habit. But when we are handed an unwanted circumstance that is inconvenient or painful to us, it can be especially hard to cultivate a heart of thanksgiving toward God.

But Scripture says God's will for us is to "rejoice always, pray without ceasing, [and] give thanks in all circumstances." God desires that we be so connected with Him—so in tune with the hope we have in heaven—that our immediate response to any situation is rejoicing and thanksgiving. No matter what. We can start doing this by cultivating a heart of gratitude through practices such as making thankful lists every day, starting our prayers with thanksgiving, and thinking of the positive things in life before we allow ourselves to list the negative.

Thank You, Lord, for all You have entrusted to me, both the good and the difficult situations. May I be a good steward of these things, being "joyful in hope, patient in affliction, faithful in prayer," as Romans 12:12 says.

REFLECTION

How can you train yourself to give thanks always? What does it look like to rejoice in the Lord—even during difficult circumstances? How do you find brightness within the sadness? And how does this change your perspective on grieving well?

R r R r R r R r

Rejoice always, pray without ceasing; give thanks in all circumstances; for this is the will of God in Christ Jesus for you.

1 Thessalonians 5:16-18

Seek the Kingdom of God above all else, and live righteously,
and he will give you everything you need.

MATTHEW 6:33 NLT

"You're so needy!" If you have ever heard those words, I'm sure they were not said in a positive tone. A negative connotation surrounds the word *needy*—we would much rather be seen as strong, independent, and secure. Neediness is a weakness we must rid ourselves of and definitely never reveal.

But neediness is just a part of the nature of our souls. We are human, and God created us with needs. In our minds, neediness can mean we are vulnerable and weak. So we become guarded and cynical, believing that if we only had more security, or pleasure, or recognition, or comfort, or satisfaction from (fill in the blank), then our cup would be filled. Yet we will never find relief through earthly things. God promises to draw close to those who are aware of their fundamental neediness and hopeful that He will restore them.

Lord, where am I being driven to fulfill my neediness? Please forgive me for chasing the temporal, Lord, and come close to me. I need You, Lord. Make me aware of Your presence and confident that I am beloved by You. Only You can provide the solution to my needs. Lord, help me open my fists and, with open hands, surrender my problems to You.

REFLECTION

Instead of trying to fulfill your needs with temporal solutions, what if you brought them to Christ? What does it look like to have your needs met by God?

Ss

Seek the kingdom of God above all else, and live righteously, and he will give you everything you need.

MATTHEW 6:33

The LORD himself goes before you and will be with you; he will never leave you nor forsake you. Do not be afraid; do not be discouraged.

DEUTERONOMY 31:8

Are there seasons in which you have felt completely isolated from the Lord? When you have not been able to hear His voice or feel His presence? Whether due to difficulty, loss, grief, depression, sin, or feeling overwhelmed, we may feel far from the Lord and afraid not only of walking in the wrong direction, but of going forward alone. During these seasons in our lives, it is important to remember that God is with us, even when we do not feel His presence. Psalm 34:4 says, "I sought the LORD, and he answered me and delivered me from all my fears" (ESV).

Persevere in seeking the Lord, and you will find Him. Pursue His heart and the things that matter to Him. This means putting down unnecessary distractions, repenting of sins that are creating a wall, and spending time in acts of worship. Whatever it is that causes you to be in awe of the Lord—whether diving into Scripture, journaling, sitting in nature, listening to worship music, studying His character, or creating—do more of that, my friend.

Lord, I feel far from You right now. But I know this is far from the truth because of Your promises in Scripture. You are with me always and promise never to leave me or forsake me. Help me be more aware of the Holy Spirit and Your presence.

REFLECTION

The best way to remind yourself that you are never alone is to write down the truth from God's Word. Spend a few minutes writing out verses that promise He will always be present in your life and place them somewhere you will see them every day. Here are some you could use:

Deuteronomy 31:6	*Psalm 46:1*	*Zephaniah 3:17*	*Romans 8:38-39*
Joshua 1:9	*Isaiah 41:10*	*Matthew 28:20*	*Hebrews 13:5*
Psalm 23:4	*Isaiah 43:2*	*John 14:16*	

The Lord himself goes before you and will be with you; he will never leave you nor forsake you. Do not be afraid; do not be discouraged.

Deuteronomy 31:8

*Understand this, my dear brothers and sisters: You must all be quick
to listen, slow to speak, and slow to get angry.*

JAMES 1:19 NLT

When my husband and I were dating, we enjoyed taking walks around our college campus. On those walks, we would talk about life, tell each other stories, and discuss our views on different subjects. And every time, as the conversation progressed, I would talk louder and louder until I was almost yelling. The worst part was, I wouldn't even realize it was happening. So, very kindly, Drew would put his hand on my arm and tell me, "I'm right here. I hear you." At first, that caught me off guard, and I felt a little defensive and embarrassed. I didn't realize how much I wanted to be heard and to feel important to someone. As time went on, my speaking loudly became a sign for Drew that I was feeling ignored. He would gently point it out to me and reassure me that he was listening.

No one wants to be ignored or feel unimportant. We all want someone to listen to our hearts. Yet haven't we all had times when we spend a whole conversation talking and not really listening at all? The Lord wants us to listen to other people well so that we may love them, serve them, and know how to intercede on their behalf in prayer.

I need You, Lord. Gently point out to me the areas where I am feeling unheard and insecure. You care about my heart and are the ultimate healer. Give me grace and humility to offer up a listening ear to those around me so that I might be Your hands and feet.

─────────── REFLECTION ───────────

How can you better listen to those around you? We sometimes become so busy with our lives that we don't have the margin to be interrupted when God brings us an opportunity to listen to someone's heart. How can you be more interruptible?

U u ll u ll w

Understand this,
my dear brothers
and sisters:
You must all
be quick to
listen, slow to
speak, and slow
to get angry.

James 1:19

Vengeance is Mine; I will repay. In due time their foot will slip; for their day of disaster is near, and their doom is coming quickly.

DEUTERONOMY 32:35 BSB

Anger is like a festering wound. When left unattended, it corrodes and destroys the body with its sickness. The enemy is constantly trying to make our hearts harder, and anger is so good at accomplishing just that. Suppressing anger just creates a reservoir of hate deep down. If it resurfaces, it will become blind rage and a desire for vengeance. But the Holy Spirit wants to soften our hearts so we can receive and feel and love. He wants our hearts to remain sensitive to discern the good He has for us.

There can be a good side to anger. God wants us to be angry and care about what hurts His heart—namely, the sin in this world. But our anger is supposed to inspire us to take action toward redemption and restoring people into loving relationships with Jesus. And, as it says in Ephesians 4:26, " 'In your anger do not sin': Do not let the sun go down while you are still angry." We are not justified when we sin in our response, no matter how horrible the act we are condemning.

Lord, sometimes in my desire to be right or to get even, I act out in anger. Help me remember that "the LORD will fight for you; you need only to be still," as it says in Exodus 14:14. Please soften my heart, Lord, and help me be sensitive to what hurts Yours.

──────────────── **REFLECTION** ────────────────

When you are angry, ask yourself the question, *What do I want to accomplish with my anger?* Answer with complete honesty. Now think through the consequences in detail. What are some healthy ways in which you can release your anger? Is any of your anger righteous?

Vengeance is Mine;
I will repay.
In due time their
foot will slip;
for their day of
disaster is
near, and their
doom is coming
quickly.
Deuteronomy 32:35

Whatever is true, whatever is honorable, whatever is just, whatever is pure, whatever is lovely, whatever is commendable, if there is any excellence, if there is anything worthy of praise, think about these things.

PHILIPPIANS 4:8 ESV

What we fill our minds with consumes our hearts and influences our choices and, therefore, our lives. If we watch a lot of violent shows on TV, our mind is more influenced by those thoughts. If we scroll through social media for a long time, our hearts may be filled with discontentment. That is why it is so important to study God's Word, spend time with Him every day, sing songs of praise to Him, and fill our minds with truth.

Every day, lies surround us. They try to take our minds captive and steal the peace we can only find in Christ. So in order to renew our minds, we need not only to avoid the lies by filling our minds with truth, but to be transformed. "Do not conform to the pattern of this world, but be transformed by the renewing of your mind" (Romans 12:2). To be transformed in Christ means that your heart aligns with His heart. You love doing what you ought to do. You offer your life to God in order that it would display His worth above yours or the world's.

Holy Spirit, work in me to renew my mind so that I might be transformed into the image of God. Help me see the glory of the Lord when I spend time with Him. I want to meditate on the goodness of God above all else. When my mind wants to exalt itself, help me remember that Christ alone is to be glorified and exalted.

─────────── **REFLECTION** ───────────

What do you fill your mind with during your day? Think about the narrative behind each of these things and what they are telling you.

Ww Ww Ww

Whatever is true, honorable, just, pure, lovely, commendable, if there is any excellence, if there is anything worthy of praise, think about these things.

Philippians 4:8

PRACTICE

*Xerxes liked Esther more than he did any of the other young women.
None of them pleased him as much as she did, and right away he fell in love
with her and crowned her queen in place of Vashti.*

ESTHER 2:17 CEV

So many times we find ourselves striving to be more and do more. Deep down somewhere there is a lie telling us that in order to serve God well, we need to achieve something great. Something big. But that is so far from the truth! God never asks us to do something big or grand or "important" in order to serve Him and accomplish His purpose for our lives. We should take very seriously the relationships and resources with which we have been entrusted. There are so many day-to-day tasks in which God has asked us to be faithful and obedient, serving Him.

In the story of Esther, her cousin Mordecai says to her, "Do not imagine that because you are in the king's palace you alone will escape the fate of all the Jews. For if you remain silent at this time, relief and deliverance for the Jews will arise from another place, but you and your father's house will perish. And who knows but that you have come to the kingdom for such a time as this?" (Esther 4:13-14 BSB). God has entrusted each of us with gifts, talents, relationships, and time that were purposed for His story. We need to be good stewards of what He has given us.

Thank You, Lord, for the life You have given me. I pray that I would glorify You with my time, talents, relationships, actions, and even possessions. Show me what it means to be a good steward of these things.

REFLECTION

What has the Lord entrusted you with, and how might you use that for His glory?

$\mathcal{X}$ x $\mathcal{X}$ x $\mathcal{X}$ x

Xerxes liked Esther more than he did any of the other young women. None of them pleased him as much as she did, and right away fell in love with her and crowned her queen in place of Vashti

ESTHER 2:17

Yes, my soul, find rest in God; my hope comes from him. Truly he is my rock and my salvation; he is my fortress, I will not be shaken.

PSALM 62:5-6

May the Lord help our souls find rest in Him alone! Many times, these are more accurate statements about our souls finding rest:

- *I search for rest in the love or approval of another.*
- *I search for rest in a clean and orderly home.*
- *I search for rest in my accomplishments.*
- *I search for rest when the kids are calm and behaving.*
- *I search for rest once I feel ahead.*
- *I search for rest by distracting myself with fun.*
- *I search for rest, but I never really find it.*

There are a million places we can (and often do) look to find rest for our weary souls. Even when we know those places will not give us the rest or security we desire, we often find ourselves pursuing them. But nothing satisfies our souls except God Himself. The Scripture says, "He alone is my rock and my salvation" (Psalm 62:6 NLT). He is the One we should be coming back to in order to find strength, security, salvation, hope, and rest.

Lord, You are my shepherd. You renew my strength and give me rest. I am burdened and constantly searching elsewhere to find strength and security. Lord, help me remember who You are. You are my rock and my salvation. As Matthew 11:28 says, "Come to me, all you who are weary and burdened, and I will give you rest."

REFLECTION

Take some time to meditate on Psalms 23 and 62.

Yy Yy Yy

Yes, my soul, find rest in God; my hope comes from him. Truly he is my rock and my salvation; he is my fortress, I will not be shaken.

PSALM 62:5-6

The LORD your God is with you, the Mighty Warrior who saves. He will take great delight in you; in his love he will no longer rebuke you, but will rejoice over you with singing.

ZEPHANIAH 3:17

- The LORD your God is with you. We are not alone. The Almighty God who has all power in heaven and earth is on our side.

- The Mighty Warrior who saves. He will rescue us. We have nothing to fear from any enemy.

- He will take great delight in you. He looks at us with the deepest love and desires to show us His goodness.

- In his love he will no longer rebuke you. He forgives us and silences all others who go against us. His affections are so strong for us that He delights in expressing His love. He makes no mention of our past sins.

- But will rejoice over you with singing. He sings over us because He is delighted in us. We are His chosen and redeemed, and we carry His righteousness upon us.

Sometimes it's difficult to imagine God loving us in such a deep and intimate way as His beloved. But it's this type of love that our souls yearn for and that we dream of all our lives.

You know my heart, Lord. I am so often broken and longing for the perfect love You offer. Help me stop searching for this love from others that only You can give. Allow me to rest in Your love, completely safe and secure.

REFLECTION

Our souls long to be loved and secure. How often do you look to others to fill a void in your heart? Do you have broken relationships that hinder you from trusting that God loves you?

Zephaniah 3:17
The Lord your God is with you, the Mighty Warrior who saves. He will take great delight in you; in his love he will no longer rebuke you, but will rejoice over you with singing.

ABOUT THE AUTHOR

Jenny Highsmith fell in love with art at an early age while attending summer camp in her hometown of Knoxville, Tennessee. Her artistic passion led to a degree in visual communication, starting her own graphic design company with her best friend after graduating college, and ultimately to opening her own print shop in 2013.

When not busy lettering, Jenny enjoys having heart-to-hearts with friends, spending time outdoors, painting, having anything to do with Christmas, drinking lattes, and going on dates with her college sweetheart and husband, Drew. Jenny and Drew live near Atlanta, Georgia, with their three children—Rowan, Conor, and Julianna.

Jenny is devoted to her faith, family, and friends. She feels that God has purposed her life for creating beauty and empowering and encouraging women to discover their unique calling.

Let's stay connected!
www.jennyhighsmith.com ◆ **@jennyhighsmith on Instagram**

Be sure to visit **www.jennyhighsmith.com/practice-sheets**
to download extra practice sheets as well as to see a video of how
Jenny hand letters the alphabet from start to finish!